God Loves Addicts Too:
A Community Book Project

Published by *A Moore Book*

Envisioned by *Bridget A Moore*

Contributions of Authors listed

with chapters

D1564017

ISBN: 9798674579021

DEDICATION

To all the survivors that have quit and their families that have endured and supported them through the journey!

To all the ones that are still struggling, I hope that these stories give you the strength and courage to change the course of your life and help your loved ones continue to love you and fight for you until the end!

To all the ones who have lost their lives while trying to quit and to their families who still live with the memories good and bad of their loved ones!

Rest in Peace

Crystal Dye

God Loves Addicts Too

CONTENTS

ACKNOWLEDGMENTS

I would like to thank each author who committed their time and their heart, while trusting me with their story. My heart overflows with excitement and tears of joy!

Bridget A. Moore

A Moore Book
.

INTRODUCTION

I am sure that somewhere down the line we have seen and or heard the famous phrase "Just Say No"! Many of us went to the school rallies and signed each other t-shirts, while vowing that we would never do such things. The fun and excitement we felt just to be a part of a movement and being in control was electrifying, not to mention we would be able to miss our fourth period class. The joys of committing and setting boundaries for our lives transformed our thinking and allowed for us to feel free-will at its best. The ironic thing about free-will, is at certain times, it can be the worst thing for you. People all over find themselves going to amusement parks, waiting in line for hours, simply to enjoy the rush of a ride that will last less than three minutes. They anticipate the fun they will have, while knowing that it will be over soon after it start. As a middle school student sitting at a school pep rally screaming "Just Say No" as loud as you can, we never envisioned there was life outside of that day and a force so strong that could change our thought process and entangle us in a rollercoaster that would not stop simply because we asked it to . We would need a stronger force to step in. Funny thing is when we said "No," we didn't understand what that entailed. It was never about the many drugs, the alcohol, the nicotine, the sexual desires, the food, the gambling, the internet, or any other addiction we managed to leech on to! Every addiction is simply the unprescribed self-medication to underlying issues that were never properly treated. The visions that we saw, the visions we never saw, the things we heard, the things that we never heard, the places we went, the places we never went, the touches we felt, the touches we never felt; The desires we had for appreciation, acceptance, self-worth; The feelings of rejection and isolation that burdened our existence. How do we undue any of these things? We shout, yell, laugh, cry, get angry, and we are still lost. We all suffer from these underlying issues, but we just can't treat ourselves...

Bridget Moore
North Carolina

BATTLEGROUND

We are always programmed to chase our dreams and fulfill fantasies from diapers to diploma. It's the American Dream, a fantasy that embarks imagination and adventure. Some of us chase these fantasies individually, and other times we chase them for someone else.

I grew up watching Teenage Mutant Ninja Turtles and imitating W.W.E wrestling. These images of being the man and everyone liking me, cultured me into the individual I am today. It was always acceptance and being liked. Always who will be my friend and love me for who I am, versus what I can do. Interesting that the "what you can do" seemed to value more weight than the "who I am", and as a child-often times didn't really matter. I always coincided the two, and hey, if everyone was happy-I was happy as well.

Reality tends to shadow fantasy as an adult, and we soon learn through trials of harsh pain that essentially human nature is selfish. Not selfish in a bad way, but more selfish in a truthful way, and this reality haunts every fantasy we imbed... It starts in childhood, and many times reveals itself, during our teenage years in high school, that we are not all that we necessarily believe we are to be.

Addiction is the topic, and being a recovered addict for many years, the true definition of addiction is fantasy. I will repeat, the true definition of addiction is fantasy...

Every addict must be truthful to self to conquer addictive behaviors, especially behaviors that have a grip on the very essence of the soul...

For me, addiction started before the drugs, and started well before college party days. Addiction started early in childhood, and the so called "substances" of my adulthood were only symptoms of my childhood pains. I was crying out for a healing when I was a child, only I didn't realize that this thirst would only be quenched with a little dose of reality.

There are some truths that I learned in my recovery, and I choose to share these truths with you in your road to recovery....

Every stage of my addiction encompassed "acceptance". It started early with acceptance issues amongst peers in school. I was always the one in class making jokes, even to the point of humiliating myself, to receive others acceptance in laughter. I mean isn't that how it works? We laugh at others in humiliation to run from the hidden insecurities of ourselves. We tend to reject the deep-down closet convictions of truth and disguise them for fallacies. Sad to say, that never changes, even into more developed areas of adulthood.

I never thought that my life would spiral into the pain I created upon myself and loved ones, inhaling that first breath of toxic fantasy. No one explained to me that the first sniff into my nostrils would never have the same effect as the next million. The drinking was cool, because everyone was doing it-and at the end of the day it numbed the pain of the monster I called my past.

Children are instructed to imagine, and these imaginations turn into fantasies that we never really accomplish later in adulthood. Now, don't get me wrong, fantasy is good, and imagination is beautiful... The problem is, and always end up being, truth in the fact that we never accomplish these foolish fantasies. It's hard to tell a child that at a young age, and even harder to tell an addict that during graying stages. Some learn by hurting others, and others never learn and hurt themselves in the process. Life is not fair, and children are not taught this horrible truth in adolescence. A wise man once said, "Truth deserves no apology". These are still hard words for me to swallow to this day.

So what makes you different than the deadly addict stages that I've accomplished in this journey we call life? We are all human and experience the same things, so there shouldn't be a difference, right? You see that's the problem, that we neglect to teach our children in adolescence. We are all human, but life tosses us different experiences, and no one's experiences are the same. What may be easy for you to handle, may be a harder for the next person.

Addicts usually fall short in one of three different categories, and I'm here to share them if you really want to understand us from a perspective of compassion. We choose fantasy over disappointment and will hold on to false realities over truth. We stumble in acceptance and want to be loved and valuable. We love to dabble in fantasies with naivety, and not believe something if it hit us square on in the face. Addicts groan for acceptance, question their worth, and refuse to accept to be loved. It's all in our perception of the fantasy, and oftentimes we choose fantasy over reality.

Disappointment to an addict, is no different than the devil to a Saint. We can experience disappointment and repeatedly refuse to accept it. Disappointment can dress itself as a wolf in sheep clothing and we will see a sheep every time. We are your strongest fighters and will squabble with anyone or anything that comes in the way of disappointing our imbedded fantasy. Truth be told, we will fight the fight of fantasy until death, and no one can save us but ourselves.

So you may ask yourself, how do addicts recover and cope with the daily disappointments of this journey we call life. My answer to you is that the survivors of this beast called addiction is only made for the strong... The ones who accept truth even in the fashion of disappointment and keep toting the torch. The ones who swallow stubbornness and starve pride. The few that replace acceptance from external forces and clutch true acceptance from self. Addicts must realize and agree that no external force can dictate worth. They must acknowledge that no one can love you more than yourself. Addicts must accept themselves despite rejection from the world. It's a confidence game that we play throughout our minds daily. A battlefield that we fight with every external element against us. A truth that we are vulnerable at all stages, because for some reason, we bit more of the apple than you...

Acceptance, worth, and love must be balanced daily for an addict to win this game we call life. In essence it is a game because our embedded fantasies outweigh everyone realistic truths. Sometimes we get so wary with this daily battle in our minds, that we need a release. We must accept this release today, the day after, and the rest our lives. Often, we faint from losing and, find something to numb the pain. Most of us survivors hold onto a truth that will get us through the day. We know that this battle will begin tomorrow, and we accept truth that we won it today. We continue to breath, and accepted truth to numb our harsh fantastical perceptions of pain...
Be blessed!

**JONAS WATSON
VIRGINIA**

THE ONE JESUS WENT FOR

In Luke chapter 15 and verses 3-7, a story is told of how Jesus left the ninety-nine sheep to go find the one that was lost. I always believed that Jesus went looking for the lost (the unsaved) sheep in this story, that is, until I realized that the sheep referred to in this story was actually me. I really did not have a horrible childhood. Actually, with the exception of a few bumps in the road, I had a good life, with a good church going family and plenty of opportunities to excel. It was only after graduation from high school that I began to venture into a dark world that I knew so little about. It began simple enough, smoking, drinking, the parties that went on all night and then suddenly, my life began to spiral out of control. Drugs entered the picture shortly thereafter and soon the drugs became my way of coping with the life I had created.

But!! This is not the real story here, after four years of downward spiraling, God graciously saved me, and my life was totally changed. I began teaching Sunday school, and later, I felt the call of God in my life to preach His gospel. I went to college and then into my first pastorate ministry. My life was amazing, and I honestly could not believe how blessed I was at the time. I moved into my second ministry in 2002 and, once again, I felt my life, with my wife and children, was perfect.

Then came the year 2005, a year I would honestly rather forget. My wife and I had grown distant but, honestly, I was so busy (doing the Lord's work) that I missed all the signs that were right in front of my eyes. What happened next is kind of a blur, an extramarital affair that I never saw coming, an angry preacher (Me) that could no longer see himself in the pulpit, two children's lives that had been devastated and a church left in pieces. It was like the aftermath of a bomb going off inside of a small room. I walked away from everything that I once held so dear. I walked away from the church, the ministry, and God. The next five years were horrible, I drank myself numb to forget the pain and laugh at the cruel joke that I believed my life to be. Darkness engulfed my world, and I became comfortable with the demonic company that I had acquired.

In 2007, as my life collided together, satan whispered into my ear and said: "Take one bullet and put it into your pistol and pull the trigger, no one will even notice you are gone." I thought about it and then decided that I didn't want to feel the pain of the bullet piercing my brain so I ended up with a gun in one hand and a fifth of Vodka in the other. At that moment, I felt no remorse, I made no phone calls (that was selfish!), all I wanted was for it to be over. I pulled the hammer back on my 357 and I felt the barrel press against my head. I felt my hand squeeze the trigger.............. Suddenly! I opened my eyes, and it was morning, and a family member was banging on the glass door that entered the room. She was frantic because she could see me slumped over and the gun hanging from my limp hand. By that afternoon, I had been placed in a Christian Rehab facility. I thought I had passed out before I pulled the trigger, however, My cousin (who is with the sheriff's department) had retrieved my gun and informed me that I had indeed discharged the gun but the bullet failed to fire. I know that God Himself put His finger in that barrel and He saved my life that day.

I would love to tell you that I did not struggle anymore after that point, but it actually took me years to forgive myself for what I had done to so many people. God finally directed me to have a funeral for my past, to plant a flower and walk away and that is exactly what I have done in my life (Praise the Lord).

Today, I have returned to ministry, my family and my life restored, and God is my King!

Question and answer time:

1. Where are you in this story?

- Maybe you are close to God and all is well. If so, never take that for granted and always remain close to the Master's side (Read your Bible, Pray and serve the Lord with all your heart)

- Maybe you are strayed away from God. Maybe you, like me, find yourself as the one Jesus had to come looking for. If so, realize that YOU may have lost sight of God, but HE hasn't lost sight of you!

- Maybe you realize that you just want to "come back home" If so, please pray this prayer with me today:

"Dear Jesus, I admit to you that I have sinned and my life is a mess but I believe that when you died on the cross, you died to pay for each and every sin of my life. I ask you to forgive me, cleanse me and help me to commit my life to you each day of my life.

In Jesus Name,
Amen

Tim Gore
North Carolina

CRYING FROM WITHIN

This is the part of my life that covers my additions with lust, alcohol, and drugs. I choose to use the name Bo Bo because of personal reasons but pray this will bless someone. The journey began around the age of 15 when I stumbled across some Playboy and Penthouse magazines. I didn't realize that this would begin a down fall in my life, but I kept on anyway. I began to fantasize about what I was seeing, and this began to fill my head with all kinds of sexual desires. I began to masturbate all the time. As I grew older, I began to have sexual relations, and something was going on with me that I couldn't control. Yet, I was a shy young man that was trying to hide what was really going on even though at that time I didn't understand it. I was so shy I didn't even ask anyone to the prom because I thought no one would go with me. I guess

I had low self-esteem issues. I was in high school and I must have been around 17 or 18 years old. I was helping a few classmates put up the Christmas tree on top of the school when one of them had a joint of marijuana. They were passing it around and because I didn't want to look like a "square", I took a puff and that's when it all began. It appeared that the feeling of being high was better than what I was feeling at first. I didn't know why it felt that way, but it did. I wasn't the shy guy anymore; I had found a coping mechanism but what was I trying to hide or what void was I trying to fill? Whatever it was, I felt important and accepted. Then the drinking begun, and I was at a place where I had accepted being intoxicated and high but was functioning. I began to think that this was the "norm" for me, and it was. I was crying but no one noticed it. I graduated high school and went into the service to run away from me but when I got there, I met the same person. Nothing had changed! Even though I left, I took me, with me. In the military marijuana was off limits as well as all drugs. Drinking alcohol was accepted and I met some of the biggest drunks in the military and I had become one of them. I had become addicted to drugs, alcohol, and sex. I couldn't get enough of either and I meant I was going to try and get enough but couldn't. The strong desire had taken control of me and I couldn't get loose, but I didn't want to get loose either. I was a grown man, and I was doing my "thing". I had begun to drink every day. I went to the extremes oftentimes getting drunk. I had begun to have more sex and the drugs had gone from marijuana to other drugs. I was being consumed by alcohol, drugs, and sex. I thought I was the life of everyone's party. I had been exposed to a world of sin and I loved it. I didn't have to feel that other way any longer. However, I didn't understand why I was crying from within. I don't know what really brought it on, but I do know it was a lack of something. I had lost a very good job and had started another job and was doing the same thing. I was abusing my own self and didn't know why. I didn't realize I was playing on devil's turf and that he was trying to kill me.

Two DWIs and I still didn't get the message. I was destroying my marriage and my children's lives because I was selfish and only thinking about me. But in August of 1993, I had got really tired of fighting these demons. I surrendered my life to the Lord Jesus because I could feel myself heading straight to hell. He heard my cry and rescued me. I asked Him to take these desires away and He did. The desire for alcohol and drugs were gone and the void was filled with the Lord

Jesus Christ, but the addiction of lust and sexual desires were still hanging around. Even after I got called into the ministry these desires were still hanging around. I had planted so many seeds through books, TV, videos and strip clubs that it was hard to shake this stronghold of sexual immorality. I taught the Word and preached the Word but couldn't stop masturbating. I was messed up. Didn't nobody know but me and God. I would do it and afterwards and say," Lord forgive me ". I needed deliverance bad, but couldn't no one help me. I couldn't tell anyone because they would have thought the worst of me. Folks would have judged me and condemned me. So I kept it to myself. This was a hard battle and a real stronghold. I was diagnosed in 2017 with prostate cancer. God had grace upon me because He didn't take me out, but I had to pay. Because I didn't stop, God allowed me to go through the treatments and He was right there with me. A part of my treatment was six hormone shots. These shots took all my sexual desire away. Thank God that my PSA levels are below zero! God, I hear You and I don't have to cry from within any longer. To God be the glory!

Anonymous

FORGED PAINTING

My story.... Where do I begin?

Major depressive disorder became my grim cloud of reality around sixth grade. Before that time, I'd say my life was average, having grown up in a typical middle-class family. My teen years were hard, having experienced both emotional abuse and low self-esteem. At fifteen, I had my first suicide attempt. The memory seems distant, but the pain still cuts deep. Experiencing near-death alone on my bedroom floor with the thought that the world would be better off without me. Those pills pained me, but I came out of it unscathed. Little did I know this would be one of many missed wake-up calls. To an outside observer, my life looked more than fine. Keeping up appearances, I excelled at school with above-average grades. I was young and worked hard to establish a path towards veterinary medicine. My prospects looked bright, despite that dark cloud that would often bare sight.

I went onto college, then veterinary medical school abroad. In a brief time, my once top grades fell low. Drinking often at pubs belonged to my new normal. It started off slowly, but progressively became habitual. Drinks most nights, cocktails at brunch, then the 'hair of the dog' slowly crept in. Blackouts became common. Being thrust into the Scottish culture that drinks and drinks more, there were no clear red flags that occurred in my mind. I must not forget my Scottish boyfriend; foolish I was for falling for him. It started dreamily, but rapidly enough he emerged into a very dark drunk. Our ending followed during one very drunken fight. There were damages left to both me and my flat. My rock bottom followed on one frigid night. Those prescription pills numbed me, but I found my genuine comfort within the depths of alcohol. Alone on my bathroom floor, I didn't contest that it might be my very last night. Had it been sheer luck that I woke some two days later, dazed and confused, still curled on that same icy floor? In the weeks to come following that night, I packed my bags and headed back to the motherland. I truly believed my pitfalls were due to lacking intellect, never considering the effects of alcohol's dark depths.

Not one to self-pity, I found work in academic research. In just a brief time, this disease again reared its big ugly head. Drinking snuck in and productivity went down, surely enough I began showing up late. The sick days too numerous to count. The results of alcohol numbed feelings becoming a safe and comfortable norm. There were countless lost nights with many blurred faces, while often waking up in unknown places. My employer eventually cut my contractual hours in half, thus finding myself on dead-end tracks. Having no place to go and feeling down on my luck, I skimmed by with my graduate school acceptance. Keeping up with appearances, I obtained my degree with an outward appearance of ease. But how could I forget those countless reckless nights? Brushing it off as things seemed just manageable enough, I seamlessly moved on to the next phase in my life. Onwards to California and the start of a new career! All new beginnings start so bright, but sure enough, those old dark patterns soon came to light. My high hopes of promotion steadily declined, as my work no longer reflected a desire to climb. As time moved on, my intellect felt smothered, and what was left of my vigor simply grew darker.

In April 2019, I was introduced to my young niece and nephew during a short weekend away. Realizing I was now a new role model, I looked to the mirror to see who was there. To my surprise, I found the reflection of a deeply troubled alcoholic. I checked myself into rehab just a short week later. Thirty days in treatment gave me a sense of clairvoyance—that sneaky pink cloud. I maintained abstinence for a solid six months. However, life never lets you get by without a test or two. You see, I lost my job just two weeks after my discharge from rehab. In the months that followed, the bills slowly piled up, job offers kept slipping away, and to create the perfect trifecta, my boyfriend robbed me and then moved away.

I relapsed in October 2019 to a very severe degree, drinking my sorrows away with a vodka bottle each day. Easily two weeks had gone by, when I realized the end needed to be near. I thought, 'This sobering up fuss should be easy enough'. Delirium tremens followed, with hallucinations that were so very real. First was the onset of gut-wrenching anxiety, followed by those tremors and shakes. Vomiting, lethargy and drenching with sweat—I showered in hopes of feeling refreshed. The next thing that followed was a deep flash of pain. I realized the lack of alcohol was causing my mess. My muscles clenched tight as I screamed out in pain and collapsed to the floor. I was panicked and oh so very, very alone. Crawling into bed, another seizure followed, I knew withdrawals could easily cause death. So, I continued self-medicating with too much fear to even be sleeping. I was in the depths of my depression and could not bring myself to get help. Another week passed; nearly certain my addiction would kill me. My delusional mind was somehow assessed just through a few mindless drunk texts. In a short span of time, the police and paramedics were at my door. Rushed to the hospital, I was placed on a 72-hour involuntary hold. With several heavy doses of benzodiazepines, I slowly detoxed off my alcohol-fueled binge.

Another thirty-day rehab program followed. Grateful for my second chance, I soaked in information at an exceptional rate. All those years of schooling had trained me for this life test. Knowledge is power; at least that's what I thought, but the application part? I very clearly missed that mark. Onwards to outpatient treatment, where I attended my first recovery meetings. I checked off the boxes on my trusted rehab guides, I thought with much confidence, 'I've surely got this right'. Funny enough, those teachings didn't get me far. Crushing debt and approaching a year without work, my ability to cope broke. My downward spiral happened once again in February 2020. With a slow but turbulent decline, I found myself in that well-known rock bottom state. Those former days of self-cutting had quickly snuck up. This time I was thankful that things didn't go as far. I was lucky enough that someone called for yet another welfare check. Recognizing that treatment of each disease independently was not showing success, a dual-diagnosis outpatient program came next. For the first time in my life, I could see the interconnectedness of depression and addiction. Intensive treatment followed and therapy resumed. Now, what about that old love affair with my sneaky friend alcohol? I finally acknowledged our goodbyes allowing the mourning process to commence.

During all those years, there were more than enough hints and glimpses that I now reflect upon as the telltale signs of my disease. However, those hardships and difficult life lessons were needed to obtain all that I gained. I have finally found freedom, peace, gratitude, acceptance, purpose, introspection, and self-awareness. During my short story that truly spans more than two decades of growth, I consistently put in the work with my many doctors and therapists. I persisted. I built my community. I learned to reach out. I developed the capability to sit with my feelings, to reflect, to question my thoughts, and rationalize my conclusions. Throughout this journey I have found that I'm only as weak as my weakest thought. I gained the power to harness and reframe those same dark thoughts. Ultimately, I realized that there is no secret 'recipe' to sobriety. I need to be an active participant in my day-to-day life, rather than being a reactive victim. I no longer try to be the person people want me to be, but the person I need to be for me. Live honestly, be responsible, and be accountable—I follow these principles each and every day. I now know this to be my truth: my disease is not my ending, but my recovery is my new beginning.

Kara K.
San Diego, California

LIFE UNEXPECTED

I never really understood alcoholism, even when I was an alcoholic. It was something I dabbled in since my 8th grade summer headed off to high school. The events I am about to share with you, is my life's journey. The journey of the many lows I had to hit before getting to the place I am now.

The summer of 2000. I was headed off to 9th grade, my sister was also graduating high school. That was an important year for a lot of us. The Millennium. My sister also had a graduation party that year that I remember having my first alcoholic beverage at. I still have the picture of me holding my very first drink. In that red solo cup, I had absolutely no idea that it was going to take over my entire life.

In 9th grade I attended a charter school where I met who ended up being somebody I chased and loved for most of my teenage and young adult years. We were head over heels, young love...ahhh. We dated on and off throughout high school. We went to Rio Grande high school where I cheered, played a little softball, ran track, cross country. We went to all the parties with most of the jock. We all drank to get drunk. I didn't really think too much of it. I was young, I thought this is what we were supposed to do, and I was having a ton of fun with my friends. My boyfriend and I would always fight with jealousy, and then my best friend and I would go find a party. He wasn't allowed to do much because of his parents' religion. They had strict rules about us being together unsupervised. By being unsupervised I mean with other adults who would make sure we wouldn't fornicate. While I was out with my friends little did, I know he was making friends with a crackhead next door. He missed my graduation because of this. That was the start of his addictions....

After high school we broke up for a good 9 months or longer. During that time I started college right away. I actually started college 1 day before graduating high school! I was a straight A student from middle school through high school.

Something I was extremely proud of and took pride in. I even received a scholarship for academics that I couldn't wait to put to use for my grade point average. I wanted to be a doctor my whole life. Something about life and the body has always interested me. It still does. So I was working towards a biology major.

After living my life and finally getting over the breakup with my boyfriend, guess who decided to come around again...yup. I got a phone call one night and it was him. So we did what we always did. We got right back together again. It was like we fell in love all over again. Oh the crazy freakin love we had for each other. I can still feel it in my bones. Little did I know during that time apart he picked up some new habits. Cocaine. I've heard of it, but never tried it. I didn't understand it at all. All I knew was weed and alcohol. The fighting quickly started all over again. We'd drink, fight, and he'd leave and go find drugs. I hated it and couldn't understand what was so important about cocaine. Why did he keep leaving me for that crap?! So I tried it. And that was a mistake. I loved it. When he found out I tried it, he was mad. He tried to protect me from it, and I went and did it. After that we slowly started snorting it together which is always a recipe for disaster. That was the start of our journey of getting lost. Losing our sight, losing each other.

We married on 8/17/2006. Ashley Salas, finally the last name I practiced writing since I was in the 8th Grade. I knew we'd marry and would have 2 kids. And we did. I wrote it in a diary I had of our crazy love for one another. We married at the courthouse. It was a rushed thing because of his parents' religion (again)but we were able to just be together around them. We could finally hug, and love on one another. We still hid our little secret of drug use from everyone. Our wedding night was a blur. We were drunk and fought over finding drugs to get high. Our anniversary was the SAME exact way. We were drunk, high, and fighting. Then... I found out I was pregnant, and it was like everything paused for a bit and I was able to live clean and sober for the duration of my pregnancy for my baby.

June 14,2007 Josiah Anthony Salas was born at 5:00pm. My first true love. I was afraid to look at him, I turned my head when my sister told me to look at my baby. I wasn't ready to feel what I knew I was about to feel when I looked at that baby for the first time. The baby I dreamed of having with the love of my life. This was such a hard labor, I was exhausted physically from the back labor, and mentally wondering if my husband was going to make it for the birth of our son because of his drug use. He did, he was there!

About 4 weeks after our son was born, I learned of "Pump and dump." Hmm...So there I was getting drunk with my husband while our 4-week-old newborn was sleeping on the couch, because I knew I could get rid of the bad milk. This, this is where my drinking really started to play a dark role in my life.

We broke up again, surprise surprise. I moved into a house with me and my son. My oldest brother moved in with me because he was on house arrest. He wasn't allowed to have alcohol in the house, did I care? Nope. I just hid my bottles in my closet. Yup I became a legit "closet drinker." During this time it was becoming obvious to my parents and everyone around me that a problem was starting to surface within me. My mom would find my bottles in my closet and have them lined up on the counter for me to see how much I had drunk. Did I care? Nope. My famous words, "I don't care." I got so bad, I'd put my bottles or miniatures in my baby's diaper bag to throw somewhere other than my trash on my way to work, but forgot to take them out and would leave the bottles in the bag for my mother in law and ex to see.

Everyone knew drinking was taking over my life. I lost my friends around this time. I was out of control. Id drink to get drunk and end up picking fights or just passing out. What fun is that?

Together again...I moved into my apt while trying to do better. During this time I've tried to stop the drinking a few times with no prevail until I got pregnant with my daughter. Finally, I knew I couldn't drink and so did my family. We all were able to breathe a little.

December 15, 2010 Aubree Joleigh Salas was born at 11:26 am. My baby girl I dreamed of you!! Finally a little girl to join our little family. My drinking started again shorty after my daughter was born. Not only was I drinking again, I also know for a fact I asked for 2 refills of my pain medication when I didn't need them. They did something different to me. Gave me a boost of energy that I didn't know could exist. It was an amazing feeling. So I had my tailor bunions surgically removed too, so I can get some refills for that also. I'd share with a coworker, and she'd share hers with me.

Things didn't work this time around with my husband. I found out he cheated on me during one of the times we were separated due to his addictions and I just couldn't get past that. So I did my own thing, and he did his and our addictions seemed to get worse even apart. All I wanted to do was drink my alcohol and find my pills, and all he wanted was his drugs.

This next part of my story I've never really spoken to with anyone other than my therapist. I believe this event changed me. I was already a mess from whatever I was dealing with before; but this one event had eaten at me for a very long time...

In 2012 I bought my very 1st house. I was so proud of myself for doing this. I've worked so hard and I finally got to call somewhere my own home. I bought that house for all the wrong reasons though. A little of me was like, "yes! My very own home!" and the other, was to do me, in peace. Somewhere where my mom wouldn't be in my business all the time. So I celebrated by drinking. I had my own house; my babies had their own rooms, and I was free. Everything was perfect in my eyes until that evening when my house was broken into. I was sitting outside in the front smoking a cigarette (yes, I used to smoke cigarettes!) talking to my best friend on the phone drinking, when I see someone I knew walk right in my house. If I would have known what he had in store for me I would have never followed him inside.

That night I was terrorized in my own home. I was chased around my house with the biggest kitchen knife I had, begging for me and my children's' lives. I could hear my son begging him not to hurt me from the outside of the bathroom door as I had a bottle of alcohol being shoved down my throat. Like here get more drunk! I was so confused for so many years about this situation. I slept with this person that night in the bathroom. I felt like if I seduced this person, he'd let us go. God knows sex wasn't something I wanted. I could hear my son banging on the bathroom door begging this person to please not kill his mom. I kept reassuring my baby that I was ok, things were going to be fine. I was trying to handle the situation in any way I thought I could. I was trying to protect my babies. We all laid down in the same bed, and I kid you not I slept with my eyes open the entire time waiting for this person to fall asleep so I could make a run for it. I did, I ran to my neighbor's house and found protection. I was confused and didn't understand why? We went to court and I didn't press charges. I believe it was my own guilt because I was sitting there drinking on my front porch when this all went down. I was confused about the sexual encounter, the judge told me it was rape, no matter how I see it. She reassured me that everything I did that night was for the wellbeing of my children. I did what I thought I had to do to protect my children from this person. As this person sat there listening the whole time.

I moved back in with my parents not long after that incident happened. My drinking escalated and I couldn't stay in that house any longer. During the next few years I got worse. WAY worse! I started lying about my back pain being just a little worse than it actually was to a pain specialist my sister worked for to get Hydrocodone 10mg. I worked at a hospital for almost 12 years in a Podiatry clinic, so everyone pretty much knew who I was because I had floated around for years and was the lead in Podiatry. So little Ashley was harmless right? Nope. Wrong. Nobody knew the secrets I had. I'd go through a bottle of 60 Hydrocodone 10mg tablets in about 2 days. Not including what a friend started giving me too on the side because she had her own little addiction. I absolutely loved the feeling it gave me. I would fly at work and get so much work done. I noticed I was so much happier when I was high too; everything was better. Things seemed to change for me. I was happy, and high, and then I'd drink a little with the pills so then I'd get super high. I had Josiah in sports, I "looked" like I was some kind of super star single mom totally rocking the independent woman life. I had a house, car, kids, great job. Nobody but my parents and sister knew the real me. Living that double life got extremely overwhelming for me and I started to slip. I started to experience withdrawal and want that was all about. Being sick at work was no joke. So I'd call in, make excuses to leave for an hour to meet my dealer down the street. Things just weren't looking good for me.

I left the Podiatry clinic because a new job opportunity had opened up for me. It was with the same company, but in Revenue operations. I was going to be a part of a new pilot operation they were starting. I was like wow! This would be amazing for my resume! During this time, I found the cheap little mini's that were named "99 Bananas." Disgusting. I can throw up in my mouth right now just thinking of that disgusting crap. I would walk across the street to the liquor store on my smoke break to get a few $1.00 shooters and drink them in my little cubby I shared with 3 other coworkers. We had it dark in there with Christmas lights, so I'd drink, put it in my purse and continued with my work. I started having problems with my managers and decided to leave. I left the company I had loved for almost 12 years. I think I was most sad that I left my doctor I worked for since I was 18years old thinking I was going to have better and it blew up in my face. I kept feeling so disappointed in myself. My schooling wasn't happening right now, I made a bad choice in leaving where I was comfortable and was valued.

I started working at another hospital as a surgery scheduler with an old coworker. She was my first lead. Someone who really took me under her wing and helped me build my way up when I was at the last hospital in Podiatry. Well, didn't take long for me to mess that up. I went to training one morning high, and drunk and lost my job that day. It was so embarrassing. Apparently, I was falling asleep on the computer, and talking out loud. They made me take a breathalyzer test and held my keys until someone came to pick me up. I let my friend down. I let myself down even more. I do still talk to this person, and I'm very blessed to have her understand instead of judge me and my problems.

Next, I started working at a local cancer center. My cousin helped me get this job. I was trying to stay sober at this point. I had too, this was just too much. When working and trying to train the girls were immediately mean to me. I asked them where I should sit, and one replied with "outside." And they laughed. They ate me alive there. The manager let the staff manage and listened to her staff's opinions instead of making her own management decisions. So guess what I started doing again. Yep, I started drinking on the job to get through my day. I hated work every single day. I started taking notes of the other staff when they'd use the restroom or have their phones out. All the things I was getting into trouble for from them, and she didn't like that much. I lost my job there shortly after that. Lol oh well. I went to an AA meeting after I lost this job. After stopping for minis of alcohol on the way.

After I lost this job, and in the process of looking for ANOTHER job, a friend and I picked up what we thought were Oxycodone 30mg. I remember this day so clear, he said, "don't take the whole thing, these are stronger than the regular ones." We were like how is that possible??? He said a friend thought the same thing and overdosed because he took the whole pill. So we cut it in 4 pieces and did ¼. BOY was he right! WOW that was something else. It was amazing! Turns out it was synthetic and was Fentanyl. I overdosed on these, and here's where it goes from bad, to worse.

My best friend got me job at ANOTHER hospital in Radiology scheduling. I was totally not ok working here from the start. I had an episode where I was hiding in the bathroom for like 2 hours, they had to have security look for me on cameras. I told them I took some pills that made me hallucinate to help me sleep, that caused problems for me in the past. They totally bought this story. I'm a seriously likable person so I'm sure I talked my way out of that one. I took my boss the bottle with my name on it and everything. My parents had to pick me up from work and take me home. But I didn't want to go home I hated hearing my mom yell at me about drinking. Because I was totally drinking on top of using Fentanyl. I began snorting it, and whatever other opiate I could get my hands on. So I had my mom take me to my sisters. My sister was mad that I was there like that considering I was with them the night before, so I left. I took off walking and fell asleep in the summertime in some nasty field where all the homeless drunks sleep. I could have been raped or killed! My sister took pictures of me this way, in the field hunched over sleeping. Totally wasted. And totally disgusting.

I needed alcohol and opiates at this point. I would stop first thing in the morning on my way to work to get my mini's and head off to work. I'd drink one on my way to work and have another during my first break. For my lunch I'd walk to the gas station and buy 2 more half pints to drink. One morning I believe I mixed a little too much. I remember French braiding a friend's hair and her asking if I was ok, I was like 'yeah, yeah I'm just tired that's all." Well I overdosed that day at my desk. I woke up on a gurney in the ER with nurses and doctors asking me what happened. I was like gee I don't know what's going on. I was so mad I overdosed at work. I wasn't even scared. My sister picked me up from the hospital and it was kind of a secret. I did a mandatory drug test that I wasn't worried about because they'd have to specifically test for fentanyl for it to come up on the panel. Do I was on leave until the drug test results came back. During this time I overdosed AGAIN at my sisters! She heard me gurgling in the kitchen, when she went to go check she found me hunched over on the kitchen floor where she began doing CPR on me while calling an ambulance for help. My sister was pregnant, and she was going through this with me. I woke up with EMT's on me, my chest hurting so bad from the compressions and them rubbing my sternum with their knuckles. They kept asking me what I took, and I refused to say and refused a ride to the hospital. I need to quit but didn't know how, as soon as I didn't have any fentanyl in my system, I'd become even more sicker than I would get from the oxycodone's. Then alcohol on top of that I didn't realize was making everything worse.

I could go back to work. I was right, the drug test wouldn't show fentanyl. I was so used to getting off everything, I didn't expect for me to overdose AGAIN at work shortly after returning. This time they upped the drug panel, and I was busted. I didn't even care, I was just super pissed that it happened again at work and I just wanted to get my crap from my desk because I knew I stashed some pills in my Advil bottle in my desk and I needed those. Can you believe this? I was madder about my pills being in my desk, and overdosing again at work, than I was about my friend and embarrassing her. How pathetic of me. Such a selfish person I turned into.

So at this point I was jobless, kid less (my mom was like no more I'm taking your kids until you snap), and I just didn't care about anything other than getting my stuff and my own selfish ways. I loved to drink; I couldn't stop the pills I didn't want to be sick but something in me snapped the last time I overdosed. I was polishing my niece's toenails when I just hunched over and stopped breathing. They thought I was kidding. So they pushed me over an that's where they see me gray and not breathing. I looked dead. My 15-year-old niece was left doing CPR on me alone while my sister ran to her neighbor's house for help since she was pregnant. The ambulance had gotten there, and they tried for a while to get me back. When I came to, I had already had a breathing tube down my nasal cavity that I quickly pulled out as well as IV's in my arm. I urinated all over myself. I died. Something had to give. Why was this happening to me. All wanted when I was a little girl was to live a fabulous life. To work as a surgical tech that I wanted so bad and to be forever happy with my high school sweetheart. So after leaving the hospital I knew something had to change. I decided to try. I missed my babies, and this wasn't the life I wanted for myself.

I went home. I humbly asked my parents for help, and this wasn't easy. I felt it in my bones that it was time. God had some pretty amazing things in store for my life once I made up my mind that I was done.

The first week of withdrawal was hard. I lived in the hot shower all day and night. My body hurt down to my toes. I couldn't eat, couldn't drink, my butt was chapped from the diarrhea. I lived on Imodium and suppository promethazine to help with the nausea that was prescribed to me a long time ago. But that wasn't enough. I'd drive myself to the hospital just for some fluids and maybe something for the anxiety I was feeling. At this point I was completely honest with medical personnel. Something I had never exercised before. My whole life I lied about my alcohol and opiate abuse. Never have I ever said to anyone that I was trying to recover from alcohol and fentanyl use. I was serious about needing the help because I was serious about starting over. I was scared out of my mind! I've lied to all my therapists in my past about everything I ever did. I went for my mom and said what I needed to so they wouldn't tell me I was an alcoholic, yet it was everyone else's fault. I manipulated everyone around me, and the only one I had fooled was myself. I appreciate my in-laws for stepping in and helping me when they didn't have to. They came and prayed for me and prayed over me whenever I felt I needed prayer. The faith they have in God I believe has introduced me to the love and relationship I have with my Lord and savior today. They'd tell me to pray and believe God was with me through everything. My mother in law took me to the ER a few times to get fluids, my sister in law took me toiletries and panties when I was admitted also. I had so many people who loved and cared about me that I had myself convinced hated me, and there was nothing but love and support.

I fought through my withdrawals for 6 whole weeks. I remember crying to my mom asking why it was taking so long for me to just feel better. I had never been that sick in the past. I'd go about 4 days of withdrawals and I would be better. Not this time. This time God was making sure I remembered every ache and pain I felt through the withdrawals this time. I had to have a Colonoscopy and endoscopy to figure out why couldn't stop. But little by little I actually started to feel better after all that...I was drinking protein shakes and doing a little better. It was around the 4th of July in 2018 that the peace in my heart started to take over. I have a picture of that 4th of July of me and my babies hugging looking at the fireworks. Something about that picture represents what our future together was going to be like from that moment forward... Like fireworks.

I reached out to a friend about a dental school she went to. I was home and thinking of all the things I wanted to do now that I was recovering and better. I was excited and anxious to see what my new life had in store for me. She told me about her school she went to and how they offered her employment right away after completing her clinicals there with their corporation. This excited me because I had always taken my kids there for their dental appointments since they had their first dental cleanings. However, I found a school that would allow me to complete the dental assisting program in less time as the other school. When I called to get info, this lady was so overwhelmingly Godly and explained to me how God sent me to her for a reason and how she was going to help me get into Oral Surgery since that's where I felt I needed to be. I messed up every opportunity working in the hospitals in the past from my drinking issues, I was like oral surgery is another door for me to do what I always wanted to do. So I went to school and completed school and worked in an oral surgery office for a year. I gained some pretty amazing experience and friendships there but knew that wasn't the place for me. Something told me it wasn't right for me to be there. And it wasn't. I walked into the dental office where I was supposed to go to school in the first place and handed them a resume. They have an Orthodontics and Oral surgery building; and guess what? They hired me!!! I started within a week of dropping off that resume. I learned Orthodontics, and they also have me helping in Oral Surgery. God is so good.

Today I'm still clean, and very much sober! 5/31/2018 is the day I decided to live again. I made a choice that day to be better. I went through some of the worst withdrawals for the longest time ever I believe to teach me something. I go through a lot of anxiety these days. I see Facebook memories pop up of my kids and I from like years ago and it depresses me knowing I was totally wasted in all those pictures. I honestly can say I don't remember my babies being that young. I feel like I didn't get to bond with them as much as a mother should bond with her babies as they go through those precious younger ages. I go through so much of that anxiousness with my son especially. He scares me, he's growing up and I know what's out there. I can only pray to God he realizes everything we went through, and it was because of my selfish choices. I apologized to my babies one by one. I explained to them that what we went through wasn't their fault, and I was sorry. It's true what they say about being blind through our addictions. We don't see real life for what it really is. Now that I have 2 years of sobriety my eyes are definitely open, and one thing nobody tells you the recovering addict goes through are all the anxieties of the hurt and pain they caused. Just know, it is the past, there's nothing we can do to go back and change a thing we did, but we can be more aware and make a better future from it.

Here I am, working my dream job. I know I'm just a dental assistant, but I get to do surgery every once in a while, and I get to put braces on little kids to change their lives with new beautiful smiles. I recently put braces on my son, I told him I wanted to do his adjustments, and make his teeth straight, so that way even after I leave this earth, he'll remember his momma made his smile beautiful. I wish I knew why God chose to save my life. That'll definitely be something I'll have to remember to ask him when I meet him one day. Until then, I'll continue to live this beautiful life he's blesses my kids and myself with!

Ashley N Salas

Albuquerque, New Mexico

MOVING IN THE FAST LANE

Growing up, when I was younger, I used to dream of having a big house, and many children. I recalled myself being very likely, and a very happy and joyful and loveable child. Although my mother only had three children. We were always joined by others and surrounded by neighbor's family or friends who used to hang out and join us together for family gatherings and cookouts.

As a child being in elementary school, I can remember people staying up partying and dancing, clubbing and playing cards or dominoes, dice. The usual stuff that you see in low income areas or government housing areas, when people and families are doing the best that they can do, trying to make a dollar out of fifteen cents. I remember seeing people, who would stay up all night hanging out and then would have to report to work the next day, and as a child all of these things that I would see in low income environments just seemed to me as regular life and everyday living.

Being the youngest of three children as the baby of the family, I always usually got away with murder in a funny sense of saying, my mom and my sisters would buy me almost anything that I would ask for. my Dad "David Lee Johnson". Who was a carpenter who was a hardworking man who loved and adored me and my family, who passed away when I was in the 9th grade, during this time my mom was recovering from drug addiction, but she never gave up the battle to win and overcome.

As I continued to make friends and liv my life I was still very much outgoing kid, I remember when I was in elementary school, and got into my first fight with a girl who was supposed to be my friend. She slapped my glasses off of my face. This was one of the first time that I understood that you have to fin for yourself no matter what happens in life.

The next thing that took place in my life where I knew I could use my power, was when this boy who was in my fifth grade class on valentine's day, walk into the school cafeteria and brought me some flowers and a box of chocolate and told me that he liked me. I was so flattered by his actions. Meanwhile everybody in the cafeteria was watching us.

As I recalled sharing my chocolate candy with my friends and giving the teacher and even the principal called my teacher classroom through the intercom requesting for me to bring her some chocolate which was so hilarious only to find out that the person who gave me the chocolate had stolen the flowers and candy from Wal-Mart before walking to school on valentine's day. The next year was a completely different experience. I moved into a new neighborhood and met new friends, that's where all the new fun began. I recalled being a part of girl scout clubs. at age thirteen. But shortly after this time I begin to lose interest in the girl scot program. I would play basketball with my friends and was the only girl on an all-boys basketball team.

This was a very fun time for me because at the time my best friend was also the only girl on an all-boys basketball team. So we would have loads of fun talking while dribbling the ball down the court. Overtime a year after the next my feelings began to increase for a childhood friend O'Neal.

We were close until the point of dating we would see each other daily, we would walk to the bus stop every morning, we would ride the bus together and play football together, his mom was a very nice lady, was always and was always kind to me "Mrs. Suzanne. His sister on the other hand could not stand me.

Maybe because of my outgoingness or maybe because of my sexiness... popularity... or maybe it was my overall confidence that I had in myself. During this time life was good and I was growing as a youth. O'Neal was the first person I gave my body too. Which at the time we thought that we were in love?

But we were just two young teenagers who attempted to have sex but never no hymen broken. Overtime my feelings begin to increase for him. but at the time, other friends, and people I knew where eyeing our little relationship at the time and wanted to date O'Neal for themselves, even a close friend who used to stay with me and my mom.

Had an eye for him as well... At some point we decided to go our separate ways and during the following summer I met a friend online and we begin to date. What was crazy is that his own brother wanted to sabotage him, while he was dealing with me. Over time our feelings increased for each other and at the same time being young I had met another fellow, who was my friend, he would help me with my homework and study with me.

We ended up falling in love. At the time, my mom was about to get married and she ended up moving to another neighbor and at that time I was so sad because I did not want to leave all my friends. This was also a very painful time for me because I had to leave the school my boyfriend was at. Many friends during this time had betrayed me. Because they tried to date the same guy as me. Which caused a lot of conflict in my life and feelings to change towards him and others as time went on, I started to spend more time with Mr. McBride. And as we spent more time together. I began to fall in love with him. The way he would greet me, the way he would hold me, the way he would lie to me, and the way he would sex my body.... Was completely enough to make my whole body and being to go insane.

I started to find myself. Doing things for him that was outside of my character. All for the love of a men, who did not deserve to have my body, I was used and abused emotionally by him and others. He would tell me that he loved me, but his actions showed differently. All I wanted was

Loyalty and respect and could not get that from him.

Which in return caused me to feel a certain kind of way about myself. I felt insecure, un pretty, unloved, needy. While on the other hand McBride was living his best life in the city of Fayetteville, Greensboro, Everywhere else he choose too... Looking back the thing that bothers me the most is the fact that he was brought up in church and never asked me about my salvation in the Lord at a time when I Was depressed, Majorly Broken!!!!!! And constantly brought Drama!!!!! I am grateful for Gods amazing Saving Grace; Theses life experiences cause me to see hoe God Rescued me time after time... The Drugs and alcohol could have killed me... But God didn't let it be So... Oh how I love Jesus because he first loved me.... Answer the call of Jesus!!!!!

When I look back over my life at the whole situation I was a black broken young Girl who did not have a clue who I was in Christ Jesus: I was in search of something and was looking for something in all the wrong people, places, and things. I would turn to Alcohol to fill a void that void I needed was God and to be reminded of his wonderful love.

Courtney R. Gillians
Fayetteville, North Carolina

MY PAIN POSITIONED ME

August 2002, I was 17 and my life was
never the same. There he was, my dream,
the one, and my heart had never skipped
so fast. I finally was ready to officially
become a woman. I can remember the
ride, he blind folded me and took me to a
secret location, it was just like I had
watched the movies. I remember how
cold the room was, but his touch was so
warm. He uncovered my eyes, kissed my
soul, and made sweet love to me. The
next day we cried and said, see you soon
as I left for college. That was 18 years
ago, and the last time I heard from him.
Do you know the emotional scars and
voids I felt at 17 years old, now only to be
on a campus, away from home for the first
time? I gave my keys to a boy who had no
hands to operate them. From that moment
there was a cycle, and I needed to fill my
void, I mean what did it matter? I had

already lost my virginity. I went from Ryan, who played me, to Jacob, which was my revenge, to Corey because he made me feel good the list goes on. Sex wasn't making me feel good I need something else something that was risky, mind blowing but had the power to make me higher than any drug and there she was my addiction, Tracey.

I once heard that we focus so much on the bait that we never see the hook. See I was so focused on my addiction that I never saw the trap ahead. That's how Satan works, he uses our pain to manipulate us. We develop a false sense of imagination into thinking that something is real. Tracey and I met at work, and I was drawn to her pretty face, sense of humor, lips, and the way she made love to me. I loved every second being with her. It was my escape from reality. We pretended to be best friends, but we knew what it was, and it excited me. Tracey was different from everyone else she made me feel like I was alive like any drug, but just like a drug it's temporary, it doesn't last, and there's side effects. I went from our first kiss to college dropout, to jail.

I had caught Tracey several times with other women, and because I had risked so much to be with her, I refused to lose again. We would get into fights, I would cry, and somehow, she would convince me that it was all in my head. I believed her because she loved me, and I was special. On Valentine's day I can remember driving her to a friend's house because something was wrong, and she came out with a ton of gifts while smelling like love spell while I set empty handed looking for something in return. How stupid could I be, but I was addicted. I could not shake the urge and sensation of being with her. I needed her to survive. When the summer was over, I went back to college, and for the first time in months we were separated. God always has a plan. I remember meeting this basketball player who was so nice, and a youth pastor. I could tell he was interested in me, but I told him I was in a relationship, and that my girlfriend was super overprotective or looking back now, controlling. It never stopped him from pursuing me, but I never gave in. He never judged me like many people did, he loved me where I was at. At the time I had a friend in college named Chasity who constantly reminded me that I was going to hell because of my relationship with Tracey. Only to find out Chasity went back and told Tracey everything and even lied on me. Chasity did everything in her power to break us up only for me to find out she had fallen for the same drug as me Tracey.

The side effect of Tracey's drug was destroying me, and Satan's plan for my life was working. See the KJV Bible says in John 10:10 that the thief cometh not, but for to steal, and to kill, and to destroy. I dropped out of college and the devil tried to steal my future. My hearing and vision were impaired the devil tried to kill my sight. I was alone and empty. This is where the devil tried to destroy me, but I am so glad that I serve a God that when you finish the verse in John 10:10 God reassures me that he comes so that we may have life.

One day my best friend Brianna and I went to go visit our other best friend Cassandra. See Cassandra went to the same college I dropped out of. I was still dealing with Tracey, but I was starting to pull away. When we arrived, we had a great time until it was time to leave, and I ended up getting into a fight and stabbed by Chasity the very friend who told Tracey everything. Brianna and Cassandra never left my side from the hospital, to jail, to court they were right there. God had given me a second chance at life. I could have lost my life, I could have gone to jail, but GOD! See God has a way of grabbing our attention even at the lowest point of our lives. See, Brianna dad always kept us in church, and one day during service I heard a small voice say do you want to heal? Do you want to be whole? That day I gave my life to the Lord at 19. I said goodbye to my drug that had become my addiction. I said goodbye to the pain that I had carried for years. I was done carrying weight that was never attended for me to carry. I met the Lord, He changed my life and delivered me from me. See like I said in the beginning we focus on the bait, being a homosexual, but we miss the hook which is hurt that led us there in the first place. I'm so glad God delivered me from hurt and rejection and healed my heart properly. Today, I am a youth Pastor in training, and I believe you must grow through what you go through. I can share my story with many people, and even though the process was hard my pain positioned me.

Brittney Joyner
Hampton, Virginia

THIS OVER THAT

As a boy, growing up in a lower, middle-class family, in a small Massachusetts town, I had always had big goals for my life. I had watched my parents struggle to make a normal life for the four of us kids. I was the second son, with another brother coming five years later, and a sister five years after that. They stayed married, always provided us with food, shelter, and clothing, and even went back to high school while I was in school. My first year of college was actually my dad's second year, at the same school. My dad always seemed to be working, while my mom only picked up a steady job after she got her high school diploma. We moved to northern Maine after my parents had lost our house to foreclosure in the early 1990s, my freshman year of high school.

My high school career wasn't bad. I was a good student, played trumpet in the band, and also joined the wrestling team. I had girlfriends, and plenty of close friends as well. I believed that I was on a good path, and that I alone could face the world, and conquer it! I didn't plan to rely on my family for much, because of the struggles I witnessed. I did not want to burden them, or anyone, with where I planned to go in life. In fact, I wanted to distance myself.

I joined the Army after graduation. I intended to travel the world and defend my country. That dream was short lived, due to an injury during Basic Training. I had some personal struggles around the injury, having to have a testicle removed as a young adult. I had trouble starting and keeping a relationship going. I began to drink and smoke pot daily. I did work full time, though, and decided to attend college at the local technical college. I maintained a good average, and kept my full-time job, burning the candle at both ends. The partying didn't stop either.

The constant partying soon caught up to me. One weekend, while out with a couple of my regular friends, we went on a mini crime spree, stealing a couple car stereos. I was 19 years old, and the only one old enough to be charged as an adult.

The number of charges, and the seriousness, put me in prison for a 10-month sentence. This was a whole new world for me. I had never imagined myself going to jail, let alone, prison!

I met my wife, as a pen pal, about 3 months before my release date from prison. She was from Farmington and decided to move to northern Maine with me. She seemed to be everything I needed in a girlfriend at the time. She motivated me to do better. She worked 2 jobs, and I did the same. In no time at all, my fines and restitution were paid off. I was going the right direction again.

With the announcement of our first child on the way, we decided to move to her hometown. I quickly got a job in retail at a local convenience store. Within a few months of working, I was offered a promotion, and became a store manager for the chain. I moved my family to the city, and we decided to get married. Soon, after we got married, our second child was announced. Things went great for several years after that. We had our third child, and had been on a couple different adventures, as far as my career went, switching companies, and starting my own snack food business.

It wasn't until 2002, that my demons reared their heads again. Working an overnight shift at a store in northern Maine, I slipped and fell during a snowstorm. I injured my neck and back and had my first experience with narcotics. For the next several years, I continued chasing prescriptions, and getting as many pills as I could get. Eventually finding the doctor who would prescribe the highest dose of the best medication. He also helped me to apply for disability. For years, I was getting more and more of my meds each month, without question, and I wasn't even taking them. I would sell my prescriptions, for an extra $3500 a month! I took my family on vacations around the state, never told them no, and I lived like a king. My addiction at the time was money and power. I felt respected by all those people that seemed to worship me.

The doctor eventually released me from his practice, leaving me to find someone to prescribe this ridiculous amount of medication that I had gotten used to. The next doctor agreed to prescribe, but he wanted to piss test me twice a week. But that's not a problem for someone who knows how to screw the system. I would just share with someone; a couple times a day when they would come and buy something. Boy, was I smart!? It didn't take long, with the high doses, for me to start getting addicted. I started selling less and less. I even got my wife to "enjoy" a weekend with me, without the kids. Again, that wasn't so smart.

That was how it started. The next 15 years were filled with devastation. There wasn't a day that went by that was not centered on getting my fix. I would sometimes lie in bed crying, until I got something in my system. The strained relationship with my wife, fighting over who got more, whether or not to buy groceries, and how we can keep this from the kids. The kids, though I thought I was being the father of the year, were neglected, abused, lied to, stolen from, and disrespected on a daily basis. I received a disability check, but the decision to pay the bills or get high was always a source of stress.

On October 11, 2016, I turned 40 years old. I had been looking forward to this day since I was young. The idea back then was, depending on where I was at in life, I would sell off everything I owned and drive around the Bermuda Triangle in a boat. I woke up that morning cried like a baby, as these thoughts came to my head. Here I was, disabled, helplessly addicted to anything I could find that day, in a rented, trap-house, barely fit for living, let alone housing my 15-year-old daughter. On days I was broke, I'd go into her room and steal $20 to get a fix. Other days, I could work enough to earn $500, but that still lead to the same outcome the next morning...I would be broke and sick, still. My relationship was a nightmare, only getting along when we were high and happy. The rest of the time, I was worried about stopping suicide attempts, and ducking hammers as they flew across the house. I would resign to breaking my furniture as a release for my anger. That makes more sense....

It took another 2 years for me to hit my rock bottom. After a six-week long battle with my wife, over her use of Meth, while I was using Meth and Heroin daily, things came to an explosive end. I woke up for work that day at 5 A.M. My wife was just coming in the door from a night out at a friend's. It got ugly. Really UGLY. In front of our daughter, the worst things that could be said, were said, and the worst things that could be done, were done. I got arrested and charged with Domestic Violence against my wife, of almost 20 years! Suddenly, I was not allowed to return home, I could not be around my only friend, who had also become my worst enemy. My entire life, what little I had left, was ripped away from me in a second.

I turned to my daughter, in my time of despair. She was witness to everything but believed that things could get better. With the support of her, and the rest of my children, I decided I had had enough! I wanted so bad to be out of the cycle I felt trapped in. I wanted so bad, to be a responsible parent for my kids. I wanted so bad, to be happy again.

I started by making a public plea on Facebook, declaring my addictions and my willingness to get help. I had never done this before, and I was always afraid to admit this to people. I really thought that no one knew what I was battling. I thought that I had done enough. I counted the hours online, getting cheers and inspiration with each post. But I had more to do. As the hours ticked by, I started planning my first relapse, because they say relapse is part of recovery. I knew everyone would understand and I could just slowly go back to using, and people would forget about my revelations. I realized I needed to act right away. I called on my aunt, who lives in Massachusetts. She is a nurse, and I hoped she would know what I needed to do next. She told me I could go to the ER and request to detox, and I could also ask for an evaluation for treatment. I turned to my friends on FB again and asked if anyone could give me a ride. It was a long-time friend, whom I hadn't seen in years, that answered the call. She came from the next town over and gave me a ride to the ER with my daughter at my side.

I spent the next 5 days detoxing in the ER. I made some sober connections and made a tentative plan for aftercare. I made it apparent to all involved, that releasing me to the streets, would result in my death. I finally understood the severity of my disease, and I was scared! I didn't want to die anymore. I realized I do have things to live for! I left the hospital and checked into a safe house, while I awaited a treatment plan at a rehab.

I found out through my kids, that their mom, my best friend of over 20 years, my partner, was not doing so well. She herself, had gotten worse since I was removed from the house. I couldn't leave her behind. I went and found her and convinced her to get help for herself. She agreed, but we decided that she would start the next day. Here was my relapse at last. I spent the night with her, celebrating the idea of a new life after treatment. After she was dropped at the

ER, I went out to celebrate on my own! Another one of my great ideas...

The next morning, on November 3rd, 2018, I found out that a room had opened up at the detox in Portland. I had been calling them for a week, to no avail. I remember the tears streaming down my face, as I threw clothes in a bag, and asked my dad to drive me the 5 hours down to Portland. Checking into that detox was one of the proudest moments I have. It was that decision, to leave everything I knew and loved, to become a better version of myself, that has gotten me to where I am today.

I got accepted into a long-term, residential treatment facility in Old Orchard Beach, Me. I attended AA and NA meetings five nights a week, and had extensive group therapy all day, every day. I wasn't only learning how not to do drugs, but how to live without them. I acquired tools to carry with me, throughout my journey in recovery, that I still use daily. I learned, and developed habits, of healthy living, including self-care.

I learned about Acceptance. Without using, and hiding from everyday problems, I learned that things are going to happen. I may not be able to control what happens, and I may not be able to fix the problems, but I can control how I react, or not react, to them. I learned that a well thought out reaction is often much more effective in overcoming a situation. Overreacting, or hiding from it, often causes the situation to worsen.

I left the facility after 3 months and entered a Sober Living house. I could reenter society, without having to feel like I was alone in my journey. I was being held accountable and responsible for my actions. I had to continue going to meetings and was subject to random testing. A failed test would result in my eviction. No ifs, ands, or buts about it.

Throughout my journey, my faith and dependence on my Higher Power was growing stronger. I had never considered a power greater than me and depended solely on what I could bring to my life. I already figured out that that did not produce the best results. Learning to do His will, instead of my own, gave my life a new direction and purpose.

Through His grace, I was able to get a good job within 3 days of moving into the Sober House. I was paid more to start this job, than I had gotten paid at any previous job. I soon had enough money saved to buy a vehicle and was approved for a car loan! This was not something that would have been possible a year earlier. The car was less than 2 years old, newer than anything I had ever bought before.

My journey through recovery has continued since then, and I continue to see the miracles in my daily life. Besides being chosen to write this chapter, I am currently enrolled in online college for a master's degree in criminal justice. I attended and completed a course to become a Certified Recovery Coach. I run a Facebook Recovery Group, with my wife, called "Recovery On The Road", with nearly 225 followers at the time of writing this. I read and share daily with my group, the joys and struggles of my recovery, because it has not all been sunshine and roses.

When I left the Sober House, I moved in with my wife, who had completed her program and had gotten an apartment of her own. I was still not legally allowed to do so and was arrested. I spent 2 nights in jail and risked further jeopardizing my legal fight from before. A coworker that bailed me out of jail allowed me to live with him. On the second night, he got drunk and knocked my teeth out, leaving me homeless, with nowhere to go. I've had several bouts of homelessness, living out of my new car, or sleeping in hotel rooms. I experienced the loss of my grandmother. This proved difficult because I also mourned the loss of my mother from 4 years earlier. I wasn't able to do so previously. I was lonely, scared, broken, and fighting to hold on to hope, but I never chose to use.

I am happy to be where I am today. I am clean and present for life's adventures. I am happy to share my journey with my wife, who shares the same recovery date. I am happy to be present and available for my kids. Through my recovery, they too have started to heal. My 18-year-old daughter has just bought a house with her boyfriend. My second son has joined the Marines. My oldest son works as a manager in a coffee shop chain. Their recovery continues to fuel my own.

I will forever be grateful to my Higher Power for keeping me alive to see a better way of life. I will appreciate the beauty that life has to offer, and value my role in it. Regardless of the struggles, I will forever choose #thisoverthat!

Michael Paddleford
Currently Living in Auburn, Maine
Recovery Date of Nov 3, 2018

WE DO RECOVER

Well my name is Tessa
I'm from Zanesville Ohio.
I was a child that had it rough.
 I was raped three times age 3 by a
stepbrother, 6 by a real brother 14 by a
guy that drugged my drink.
 I got depression and anxiety from, it tried
counseling then I just got lost.
I first tried pot when I was like 16 didn't
care for it so that stopped right away.
Few years later my ex-boyfriend asked me
if I wanted to try coke, I was like ok but
what it feel like he said it makes you feel
great we'll I started coke at the age 17
until I was 20 1/2 we broke up ... I met
my ex-husband in 2007 we got married in
September of 2007 and I was off to
California the army base well everything
was great I was clean for a few years
pregnant for my oldest so that's my "lil"
army brat had him in 2009 shortly after

he was born I left my ex-husband stayed in Kentucky until my son hit one moved back to Ohio what you know I meet up with all the old friends and started using coke again stopped when I found out I was pregnant in 2011 well in February 2011 my son turned 2 on the 15th he goes to grandma n grandpa's house for the night February 16,2011 I go get him and go home and called my mom asking her to go to the hospital with me they told me I was having a miscarriage I thought my world has ended I didn't start to use again until after my DNC I hated everyone and anyone the father of my second child broke up because I didn't wanted to talk to no one I felt like God hated me so I started using again for about 2 years then got pregnant again I had. Healthy little boy now at this time I'm a mom of two boys used off in on from 2013 when my youngest son was born ... Got with a "pipe-liner" had money whenever I wanted we used together and he would use being out of town and when he was home we'll I went to jail on October 12,2018 that's the last time I ever touched anything I ended of getting help rehab like I needed and was supposed to do 2 yr. felony probation I only end up doing a year I got off early I'm still with the same guy the "pipe-liner", good news about that is he doesn't pipeline no more and is clean I made him quite pipeline after I got sober to work on our family during the whole time of my use by the grace of God I never lost custody of my boys I will be 2 years clean on October 12,2020 I'm very proud of myself the person I become today I have a great relationship with my family and coworker family my kids and boyfriend I work full time at one job and part time at the other that's my story

Tessa Maston
Gainesville, Ohio

DERAILING BEAUTIFULLY:
A MEMOIR BY RACHEL TURNER

It was the 90's in the mid-summer when my whole life had changed. We had a little part in the trailer park where I grew up to do Karate. We did this several times a week. I thought it was cool to learn and to waste my time. That day we went back to his house. I didn't know what to expect, but I went anyway. We went back to his room and that's when things became scary. We were talking one minute and then the next he was between my legs. My body was doing things that I have never felt before. It was shaking uncontrollably, and I couldn't make it stop. I just keep saying it will be over soon. I was so young, and I couldn't figure out what was going on, so I felt like I peed all over myself. He whispered, "Good job Baby girl, you are now a woman." "You did great, I love you." Soon after this I began my addiction.

Well let me take you back to where it all began. When I was a small child, I can remember incidents between my mother and father. They drank all the time and alcohol was the norm around our home and amongst family and friends. One incident was when we lived outside of Grifton and dad came home drunk like always. He started on my mom as soon as he came in the house. Yelling at her. Screaming asking why certain things hasn't been done around the house. I can remember hiding as soon as he started. He slapped my mom so hard that she hit the ground. I was crying and so very scared. I wanted to help her but what could I have done. This happened more times than not. Another incident was when dad came home again and slapping her around wasn't getting him the satisfaction he wanted. So, he takes her by the neck and dangles her from the wall. I came screaming out "leave her alone, Mommy"! Just as quickly as it happened it stopped. I went outside one night looking for my dad because he had just got into a fight with my mom. He was laying at the bottom of a big tree passed out. I called out to him several times and he never answered. So, I just laid down beside him and held him. Daddy was very violent with my mom. My mom met a man a while later and when dad found out he was livid. He loaded all of us kids up and went where she was at. He pulled in the driveway and my heart began to beat so very fast. I just knew this wasn't going to end well. Dad looked back at us and told us to stay in the car and not to get out. So, we did. As we sat there scared to death, we could hear glass breaking, doors slamming, so much chaos and screaming. Dad came out with blood and sweat all over him like he was fighting someone in there. At this point I knew My Mom and Dad were never going to be a couple and that family was it. Daddy met someone new while mom was in VA. She was so great. Every time daddy would take that belt off you could literally hear it hitting every single belt loop. We would always run from him. But his girlfriend at the time always ran before him and wouldn't let him get to us. Mom was telling us that she will be back soon to get us, but we told daddy that we wouldn't leave him alone but when Mommy pulled up that day, we all got into the car and left for VA.

Well here we go to Va. Things were rocky right from the start. I swear he didn't like us. We were always in trouble and Mama never helped when he would punish us. Mom was always drowning in a beer or whatever she could get, and Her Husband always drank Thunderbird. I felt like we left one mess right back into another, nothing changed from home to home much at all. I saw my oldest sister come home one night so tore up mom, put her in a cold shower and smacked her in the face. When my mom's husband found out my little sister and I were smoking he made us chew a whole plug of tobacco. It sucked so bad. My little sister was getting so sick. I felt so responsible for this because she wouldn't have done it if I didn't give it to her. He also used to chase us around the house with a taser to scare us straight. I will never be right around a taser. They scare me so bad. Mom never said anything to him about us children. Mom was very absent back when we were growing up. She was there just not there. My mom smacked me in the face one time when I told her I would call DSS on her. Hit me so hard that I fell on my back. I never went to my mom with mess anymore. I drove her to the store one time she couldn't drive. I told her I was scared and didn't want her to drive. So, I did. Dinner always sucked at home. My mom's husband made us eat everything on the plate know matter what it was. If we got sick, we were going to eat that too. He would also make us clean ALL the time and it had to be clean. I swear he hated me, and I hated him. We were always grounded but mom would let us play if we were back when he got home. We moved into a trailer park that became a horrible memory to me. This guy that lived there was a karate teacher and had a little spot in the woods to train us kids there. I was around 10 when all this began to happen. It started with just pictures and little videos. I wasn't sure how to feel about the whole thing at first all I knew I was getting attention whether it was good or bad. Seeing him many times a week. I began to fall in love with this man. He soon became very important to me. He did many sexual acts with me and penetrated my body often. He had three stepsons living with him and they began to be a part of the abuse as well. All three of them would be in or on me in some type of way. I began to feel very nasty, but my abuser just kept insuring me this was ok and that we loved one another. He took me into the boys' room one day and told me to undress. So, I did. Piece by piece I took the clothing off. He motioned the boys to touch me everywhere. The boys started to lick between my legs and all over my chest. When the oldest boy touched my breasts, he began to erect. My abuser then made him get on top of me and penetrate me. The pain of penetration hurt so bad. I thought he was going to tear my insides out, the oldest came inside of me. The abuser came over to me and kissed me on my cheek and said I did great. This became the norm for me. I told him that I was scared each time something happened, but he just rubbed my hair and ensured that everything was ok. At that point I began to feel modified. He would always say this is because I love you. I loved this man that showed me how to be a woman, He was my best friend and lover. I loved him and I would do whatever he asked of me. I hated to orgasm so bad I would squeeze my insides just so I couldn't cum. He would always say this is our little secret. I can hear his voice as plain as day. He would also say if I told anyone that they would take me away from him and I didn't want him to go away. This went on for a while before I finally told someone. It was an adult friend of mine and I was so scared to say something because I didn't want him to get in trouble. When I told my friend she soon told me my mom and the next thing I knew he was getting arrested and I was in tears. The only man to show me love was leaving, and I just couldn't understand why. I was so lost, mad, confused, and heartbroken that they took him away from me. Well we soon went to court about it and I had to take the stand against him. It hurt. My body was shaken, and I was scared. Then he was convicted of so many counts of child abuse. Things changed for me after this. I became rebellious and wasn't listening at all to my parents, my mom's husband wanted to send me to reform school. Luckily, my Daddy came pulling up in his big rig and took me with him. We lived on the road for a bit and it was great. We went to so many places and it was so beautiful. We settled in Grifton again and I started school. I was in the sixth grade when my behavior started another turn. I wrote a suicide note to the SRO officer at that school and she called my dad. My sixth-grade teacher was always there for me to talk and such. She helped me out of many anxiety attacks. I was very troubled. While I was going to school there, I witnessed someone get murdered right in front of me. My dad and some family and friends were drinking and just having some fun. One thing led to the next and these two guys were fighting and one of the guys had the other in a choke hold. Everyone kept saying let him go let him go he can't breathe let him go. When he let him go, he fell to the floor? I was crying out loud and I was so scared. I just witnessed a murder in my home in my kitchen. The cops came and there were so many of them. They had so many questions. Daddy said to tell them I was in bed when it all started. Then I had to speak but thank God it wasn't in court. The guy wound up being charged with murder and he went away for a while. I am not sure how long he got. The counselor at my school began to do things with me and took me places. I had so many bad dreams almost every night. Life was getting so hard to deal with. Till this day I still freak out when I see someone in a chokehold. It terrifies me. I hated the vision, the dreams, the flashbacks right in broad daylight. I was 13 and living in fear already.

Soon after that I moved to Ft Campbell KY with my oldest sister. Her husband was in the military. I tried making a fresh start their living behind all my past. I started School out there and helped my sister with her baby. Everything was going good right then and I loved it. My sister worked night shifts and I would stay and help watch the baby. On my 16 birthday I got drunk with my sister's husband while she was at work and I have no idea what happened. But I slept with my sister's husband. Once again things changed. My sister hates me. She was calling me all kinds of names. Chased me all over base. But I told him to stop and this isn't right. I moved in with a friend there around the area. She became a big support in my life and helped me so much. I loved her. I stayed with her a few years and got married to my first husband. He was also a bad guy too. We fought all the time, drank and did drugs every day. He was very demanding. I didn't want to have sex one night with him and he didn't take no for an answer. He did what he wanted and when he wanted. He rammed it inside of me so hard that my eyes cried. He had put his hands on me as well. We weren't even married long. After my Dad put him in a choke hold on the truck soon after I separated from him. See a pattern yet. I am doomed. I fell down a long, big black hole after that. I did some escorting and lived on the streets for about a year. This part of my life was so dangerous and scary. People have pulled guns on me, through me out the car, and I don't know how many times I was raped. I made good money though and sex has always been my tool. Then I moved back to NC where I met this woman and we just clicked. She made me happy. We were going out about a month and then my dad found me cutting and sent me away to NY with my cousins for about a month. She called me while I was there. She told me she was pregnant and wanted to know if I was going to be there for her. I told her of course I would. The docs told me I couldn't have any kids maybe this was my way to have a child. So, when I got back from NY, I was always there through everything that she went through. I didn't leave her side. We had a baby girl; p and she was named after my favorite movie. We were so in love with this baby girl. We were doing good but then like always my life changes for the bad. Not sure when it all started but her dad began to do sexual favors towards me, and I received so many things in return. I had horses, went on a cruise, went to trail rides and rodeos, we even started a small business. I was also high every part of the day and he supplied that as well. Whatever I wanted. All he wanted was to go down on me and rub my chest. Why was I addicted to this kind of life? I felt nasty and unworthy. But it just keeps going on in my life. I hated lying to her and doing things behind her back. She meant so much to me and I failed her to. It was normal for me. I hated men but then again, they kept being right there at my side being summoned for what they wanted. This went on for a couple of years or more. Then this guy came out of nowhere one day and came to drink with my girlfriend and me. I loved his company. So, I had him on speed dial, and he came over often. We began to talk about everything. I Told him what was happening with her dad too. The more we talked the closer we got. One weekend I went with him and never came back. Went and got my stuff that morning. I Tried to tell her what happened between her dad and I, but she didn't want to hear it.

We were so close in the beginning. He even lost his job because he wanted to stay home with me. I just knew this was my soul mate. Well a couple of months in it began. The controlling as well awesome other things. My best friend and I cut up one night. He and her boyfriend wanted food, so we got them some and dropped it off at the mailbox at the end of the path. They were not happy, and we didn't come home till late night. We were drunk and high as hell. Later he called and told me to come home. Soon after we head home. All three of us were torn up so somehow, we got to talking about a threesome. So, we began to do it and when she started touching my boyfriend. I said nope and quit it. We started going outside and we walked across the yard and my boyfriend was already starting his mouth. He pushed me and then I called 911. He knocked the phone away from my ear and he began to get on top of me and punched me over and over. I couldn't do anything to make it stop. I just kept asking God to just have him knock me out. But he never did. Blow after blow. It felt like he was crushing my skull in with each hit. Finally, my best friend got on his back and began to pound on his back and wherever she could get to. Finally, he quit, and I ran inside her house because it was the closest. I was crying hysterically and rocking back and forth on the bathroom floor. It felt like it took the cops a long time to get there. They were asking me questions and my mouth wouldn't speak. I was in complete shock. And when they arrived, they took me to the ambulance and then I went to the hospital. They told me that I had a concussion and many bruises. When I got out of the hospital the next day, I called my mom and told her to come get me and what had happened. So, I went to VA for a bit of time. When I got back from VA, I was ready to get this trial over with and put him behind bars where he deserves. I was so scared to even see him in the courtroom. I began to be back on drugs hard and heavy after that. I was living so reckless. Sleeping sideways in ditches, out in the middle of the fields, and just doing whatever I could to make the pain go away. I was just existing in life and at that point I was ok with that.

The closer his release date came the more I wanted to talk to him. Crazy right? And again, I went back with him. Staying here and staying there. Living our lives very crazy. We soon moved in with a cousin of his and I became pregnant shortly after. I always wanted kids and I knew that this was a miracle that the lord had given me. This was going to be great. Dealing with his moods and having to chase him down the street to make him come home. It was very tough. Even had to break up fights for him. We wound up moving out right before we had our daughter. We had our first baby in Feb 2012 and the moment I laid eyes on her the whole world began to fade. I was in love. His' temper felt like it was getting worse and worse. I couldn't even go anywhere or do anything. Later that year my dad put a wedding together for my husband and eye. It was so beautiful. But the temper of his just kept getting worse. He ripped my night gown off demanded sex, but I pulled away from my nightgown and I hid under the steps in the back until I knew he was asleep. Then one evening in his drunken wonder he decided to talk crap to a very dangerous guy, and he didn't even care what the consequences were. Thank goodness my husband gam came to get us and brought us to her house. When we got home the next day his truck was smashed all in with a baseball bat and the windows were knocked out to. The front door was also beat in as well. And I said "You know you are going to get us killed or you one day why can't you just keep your mouth shut. 'Everyone always cleans up his mess, so he never gets to learn from them. I was always isolated from my home. He made me feel like no one liked me. When he had friends over, I wasn't allowed to look them in the eye. We had three kids all together and it just seems to get worse. I was bound to his demand. I was ordered to do all kinds of things. When things got bad, I would hide outside or go sleep with my kids, but I wouldn't do that too often because he would wake them up. A couple of years there give or take we moved in with My dad because he was sick, and his wife had left him. So, we moved in with my daddy. He was diagnosed with colon and lung cancer and had to take his treatments. My dad was very depressed at this time and he didn't have a lot of fight left in him. We were making it work though. We had plans to get my husband gone and my daddy was going to help me get back on my feet. It was three months now and he was just very tired and weak. I began to see my daddy giving up. He didn't even want his grandbabies in the room around him. My daddy was dying and there was nothing I could do about it. Everything I did or said didn't even matter. The last week he was on this earth I tried to make him go to the doc but he wouldn't and he went in on that Friday and when I got there that afternoon they put him in a coma because he body wasn't doing right. The Doc said we have tried all we can but only 17 percent of his lungs were working, and he also had an infection. If they keep trying, he will lose his extremities. We all talked about it and thought it was best if we just let him go. So that Sunday at 340 pm he left us. My dad was only 59 years old. He wasn't gone for 5 min and I already missed him. The pain of losing my daddy is something I will never forget. It hurt me. My insides were screaming his name so loud I thought that everyone else could hear it. He was my best friend, my dad, and the link to my heritage. I felt even more alone now. My life at this point began to crash and once again my life changed. A year or so later my oldest daughter at the time (6) came to me and said that daddy had a new girlfriend. Told me the women's name and where she lived. Something in me broke and all I could see was blood. I wanted to kill him and even had thoughts on doing that. Everything that he has ever did just came to me at once. I hated him. He went behind my back a month after my daddy left me. Unbelievable right. I began to put my hands on him, and he called the law each time. But I didn't care. DSS became involved in our situation and they wound up taking the kids. At first it was with family, then they put them in the system. Because I was already on probation and had cases that were convicted, they locked me up in June 2018 I became very close to my higher power and HE showed me who was there and who wasn't. It was very hard sitting with self and seeing each day go by. I tried to kill myself in there, but my higher power had different plans. I pulled a hundred and twenty-nine days in a county jail then went to Black Mountain Treatment Center for rehab. I spent three months there and began to start loving myself. The staff there is amazing, and the counselors are the best. They build you up and they let you see what's on the inside of you. They make you feel worthy and you matter. I picked crocheting there which was cool. One of the ladies taught you to do it. It's a very good mind exercise. That place made me feel like I could do what I needed for my family and more. They were very supportive. When I got released in January. I had a plan. My mom and her husband came to pick me up and I headed home. It wasn't long after I got home, and my husband was doing the same things. I stayed as much as I could to help him get his life together and get on the path I was living now. But whatever I tried never mattered. He was too busy with that street life. Each week I was only able to see my kids two hours at a time when I first got home. So, each week I made them something and brought it to our visit. I couldn't give them much, but they always had something from me each week. When I left my husband a couple months later. It was a long time coming and really needed to be done. I was about to be done with him for good. I knew I just had this. I began to see my kids much more. The foster parents that my kids were with were great. We would meet up for soccer games and park time and school activities. They were all very supportive of what I was doing. Finally got me a job and found a place for rent. The job was with a local landscaping company who gave me an opportunity. He pushed my limits every day and always showed me what I can do better. Then soon after someone gave me another opportunity and I had a home for my babies and I. Thanksgiving of 2018 the kids finally had a chance to stay with me for a couple of days and things were going great and my babies would soon be coming home. I had received everything I had been asking for. My life was complete. Before the kids came home, I moved again to another house behind my co-pastor to help with his mom and dad. Beautiful neighborhood, safe environment, plenty of room for the kids and me. I was so excited and just knew this was going to be my spot for a while. My church has always been a stronghold in life, and I felt that so much with them. They stood by me at my worst times. December 19 my kids came home. Being a full-time mom all over again and learning how to be a sober mom would be a task. But it was getting ready to be real for me. Ds made that Christmas the best they have ever had. We were so blessed this Christmas Day. Life was so good for now went to my pastor's house often and spoke with them and she always helped me out. They made me feel like a family I never had. They showed me what God love was and were truly there for me. I called her my church mom. She was very supportive of me and every time I would put myself down, she would always say something positive. I opened to her about things I never told anyone, and I became vulnerable to her. She showed me how to act like a lady and not having men drooling over you. She just showed me so many things. Being a single mom of three kids was very hard. But then in March this Covid comes and disrupts everything. Attitudes start to change, and things begin to feel different. I could feel them not liking me. I tried my best to be a Christian and live the way they lived But I could never be enough. Living each second of your day battling Anxiety, Depression, Bipolar Depression, and PTSD is very hard. I had all I needed and wanted. But no matter how happy I tried to be, it never worked. My mind would constantly tell me that I didn't deserve what I had. It will only be a matter of time before it comes crashing down again. My mind is like my own little hell that I could never get out of no matter how hard I try. It feels like sometimes there is a bag over my head, and I can't get out of it in time. I haven't been with anyone since I left my husband because I don't know how to handle what's inside first and that must be dealt with soon. I want to find love without sexuality being the first for me. I have been so damaged I don't even know if there is someone for me. It is hard being a mom that everyone else wants you to be. I was doing my best but obviously it wasn't enough. My mind just can't wrap around the goodness that is in front of me. I know I deserve every blessing God has given me but it's like my mind craves the bad. Pain is like an addiction for me. When I'm not experiencing it my body and mind goes through withdrawals. My children are the only thing I need in my life. I am far too damaged to do anything else. God will put the right man in my life one day. I soon found out that I will have to leave this place soon and go on my next adventure. Good things come and then the bad just must be right around the corner. I just want my kids to be happy and healthy and be ok. Now with this new journey I'm not sure what's next for me. I feel like the people I have looked at the most kind of turned their backs on me. Yes, I am not the best housekeep or mother even but just getting out of bed every day is an accomplishment. But there is one thing that I do know. I Will not let the evils of this world consume me. I will not go back to the life I used to live for no one. My babies need me, and I will never ever let them down again. I have so many supporters that are backing me and helping me get where I need to be. I have great hopes and dreams. This is so much more of my story. I want to help others like me and show them just to keep fighting that fight and don't ever give up. If you have a brain like mine trust me, I understand but always try to leave a little positivity somewhere in there.

This last little bit is for my mom. She was a bad alcoholic when I was growing up. She always had a beer or something in her hand. She was hiding behind so much pain. But she never showed us that pain. She covered it daily with alcohol and drugs. It would even look like she was getting abused. It was that bad. When she was with my daddy, he was very abusive physically and mentally. She would never back down to him no matter what he did to her. I guess if she was numb, she wouldn't have to feel any of it. She did her best with us and shielded us as much as possible. When my mom and dad split. I just knew that things would change but they never did. She seemed so unhappy. I can remember one time when she was passed out on the floor, my stepdad kept hitting her in the face to try and wake her up. I thought he was hurting her. She was a drop down and even hit her head several times. She drank for a long time like this. Until one day she just stopped drinking and that was about 15 years ago now. My mom shows me how to be a fighter. She has a mind like mine, but she still does what she needs to do to be where she is now. She is a warrior and has overcome many hardships in her life. She is my inspiration, my stronghold in times of trouble and foremost my mom. She stands up to life like no one I have ever seen, and she never gives up.

Rachel Turner

Eastern North Carolina

ABOUT THE CONCEPT

Bridget Moore, the founder of A Moore Book, published her memoir God please save an addict like me in October 2017. Her book shared the struggles and challenges that were faced on her journey to recovery. This book went on to encourage others as they were able to relate to the same pains that have plagued her. Three years later God gave her the vison of The Community Book Project: God Loves Addicts Too. The concept was derived from her original memoir of others helping others while helping themselves. This book allows for various people to share their story, their way without hesitation. Every story may not relate to everyone; however each story relates to someone.

Made in the USA
Middletown, DE
10 December 2020

27239417R00066